THE POCKET LIBRARY OF GREAT ART

Plate 1. HENRI DE TOULOUSE-LAUTREC. *Courtesy Ludwig Charell*

HENRI DE

TOULOUSE-LAUTREC

(1864–1901)

text by

SAM HUNTER

Associate Editor,
The Pocket Library of Great Art

published by HARRY N. ABRAMS, INC., *in association* *with* POCKET BOOKS, INC., *New York*

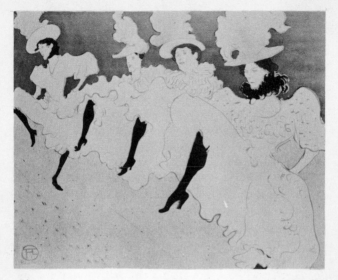

Plate 2.   MLLE. EGLANTINE'S COMPANY. *1896. Collection Charell*

Count Henri de Toulouse-Lautrec's life was brief but arresting. He was born to a family of landed gentry whose line went back to the time of Charlemagne, but he preferred the company of disreputables and lived out his life in the pleasure haunts of Montmartre. His taste for the picturesque may well have been an aristocratic legacy passed on by a quaint and autocratic father. The elder Lautrec's consuming passions in life were hunting and extravagant, story-book costume. For his son he outlined at an early date a program of horsemanship, falconry, and supervision of the family estate, but he lost further interest in the boy's development when the delicate, rachitic count fractured both legs in childhood accidents, and it became clear he could never endure a strenuous physical life.

Lautrec's bones never mended properly, and his physical deformity—a fully-developed torso on puny, shrunken legs—always made him an object of public curiosity. He found refuge, and artistic inspiration as well, in the music halls of Montmartre which he began to frequent shortly after his arrival in Paris in 1884. From that date until his death in 1901 he was a familiar figure in the various *cafés chantants,* cabarets, and dance halls where he had a special table and observed and steadily sketched the performing clowns, dancers, and singers. In this milieu he was accepted without repugnance and was enjoyed for his facetious talk and bubbling high spirits. In the ten years of artistic maturity between 1889 and 1899, he produced a prodigious number of drawings, lithographs, posters, and paintings. His appetite for work was matched by a fierce appetite for life which only Montmartre fleshpots seemed able to satisfy. Ruinous dissipation finally produced a complete mental and physical collapse in 1899, and he died of a stroke less than two years later, at the age of thirty-seven.

In the formation of his novel artistic style, Lautrec's life was a major factor, and it is impossible to consider his career apart from it. When he first came to Paris in 1882, he was taken in hand by the deaf-mute Princeteau, an academic painter of horses. Princeteau introduced his young charge to the theater and the circus, and probably did more to stimulate his

Plate 3. JANE AVRIL: "LA MELINITE." *1892. Oil*
Wildenstein and Co., New York

Plate 4. TANDEM DRIVEN BY COUNT TOULOUSE-LAUTREC. *1884. Pencil*

sense of life than to shape his artistic tastes. Subsequently Lautrec attached himself to the ateliers of Bonnat and Cormon, two other academicians; at Cormon's he met such unconventional spirits as Vincent van Gogh and Emile Bernard, and passed briefly under the spell of Impressionism. His own personal style began to crystallize, however, only in the atmosphere of the music halls.

Lautrec made his debut as pub-crawler and observer of low life at *Le Mirliton,* one of the first *cafés chantants.* The cabaret was run by Aristide Bruant, who became a subject of many posters (plate 29); and in it was hung Lautrec's first exhibition. Bruant apparently had a tremendous impact on the impressionable young painter. He was famous for his slangy songs about sots, prostitutes, and degenerates, and for a successful social formula of *engueulade* — a technique of disarming his customers by directing a stream of abuse at them as they entered his café. The *engueulade* may have predisposed the development of Lautrec's own mocking pictorial style. And Bruant's public advertisement of fallen lives, in song, also might have suggested that brisk showmanship could enliven even the most melancholy subject matter.

The determining artistic influence on Lautrec was Degas, whom he also probably met in 1884. He never had more than a nodding acquaintance with the misanthropic, older artist, but profoundly admired and studied his work. Degas' relation to Lautrec was something in the nature of Flaubert's to Maupassant. It was the difference between the unchallenged master of realism and the eager young disciple; and between the controlled, deliberating classicist and a more vola-

Plate 5. MOULIN ROUGE: LA GOULUE. *1891. Poster*
Museum of Modern Art, New York

tile and perhaps more superficial temperament. Degas provided a new storehouse of unromantic imagery drawn from actual life, and a compressed form that seemed more faithful to the abrupt movements and stepped-up rhythms of the modern world. Through him, too, Lautrec learned to appreciate the succinct shapes, expressive outlines, and dramatic color contrasts of the Japanese print.

But like Maupassant—whose art his own so closely resembles in flavor and in pithiness—Lautrec was not at home in the imposing classical discipline of his admired master. What he took from Degas he altered radically according to his own artistic needs. He reduced Degas' elaborate figured tapestry of bodily movements and counter-movements to a formula of drastic silhouettes. Always primarily a draftsman, Lautrec expressed his vision in aggressive outlines on flat surfaces. His relation to his subjects is more physical, his characterization of incident more audacious.

Lautrec's most significant contribution was in the poster and color lithograph. Between 1892 and his death he produced more than 300 lithographs and thirty posters. In these he achieved a freedom of linear improvisation, a boldness of attack, and an originality with expressive color that have not been surpassed. His resourcefulness in the graphic media allowed him to reproduce his subjects with a stylized flatness and still to characterize them, psychologically speaking, in the round. The restrictions of the media melt away before Lautrec's concise, epigrammatic style. He had a genius for excerpting some unflattering characteristic of his models and stating it with utmost economy. In a famous lithograph of the chanteuse Yvette Guil-

Plate 6. LA GOULUE AND VALENTIN. *1894. Color lithograph*
Collection Ludwig Charell, New York

bert (plate 7), delivering a popular song he evokes all her ghoulish style in the detail of her stringy, black gloves. Lautrec makes them her trademark.

Lautrec's career spans a period of transition in painting between the triumphant collaboration of art and life that the Impressionists celebrated, and the preoccupation of the modern artist with art's own processes — with experiment in medium and with interior worlds of fantasy. A sheer delight in gross human comedy enlivens even the most arbitrary conventions of his rather schematized art. Yet his vision is special; the soulless vitality of the garish, nocturnal world which he explored, and his formulation of that world, are artificial. In it the sun never shines, and goodness is severely eliminated.

In mood he is closer to our time than to the commanding creative personalities of his own day like Degas, Cézanne, and Renoir, who had a capacity for continually enlarging their artistic personalities in life or in the art of the past. Lautrec's unique vision marks him as one of the first modern artist-exiles and connects him with such other Post-Impressionists as Van Gogh, Seurat, and Gauguin. Van Gogh, the passionate pilgrim, transfigured nature into symbols of a private exaltation; Seurat lavished the pictorial science of Poussin on an artistic, wonderland world of puppet-like figures; Gauguin, the self-created exotic, tracked his soul down the remotest byways of civilization. Lautrec is perhaps the most arresting and extravagant of these sublime originals. He outlawed himself in the Paris underworld of pleasure and conferred on the inconsequence and dreariness of soiled lives the supreme consequence of vital art.

Plate 7. YVETTE GUILBERT. *1894. Water color*
The Museum of Albi, France

Plate 8.   MLLE. MARCELLE LENDER. *1895. Color lithograph*
Museum of Modern Art, New York

COLOR PLATES

PLATE 9

Painted in 1882

YOUNG ROUTY

Kunstmuseum, Basle, Switzerland

Oil, 23⅝ x 19¼"

A remarkable portrait for a boy of eighteen. It was probably painted in the garden of one of Lautrec's country homes at Céleyran or Malrômé. It is an Impressionist exercise, full of vivacious brushwork and dappled light. The expressive accents of the taciturn head, however, already suggest a forceful artistic personality and prefigure Lautrec's dramatic feeling for type.

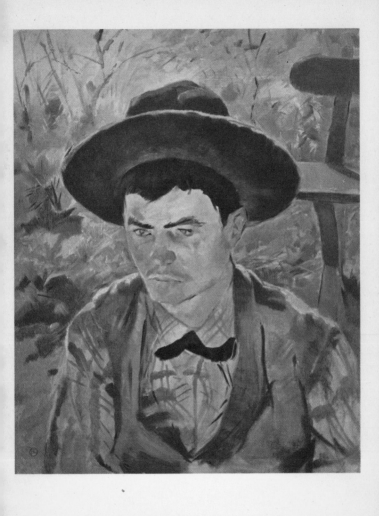

PLATE 10

Painted in 1887

PORTRAIT OF THE
ARTIST'S MOTHER READING

The Museum of Albi, France

Oil, 21¼ x 17¾"

By this date Lautrec's style was on the threshold of maturity. He still defers to Impressionist technique and atmosphere in his fleeting effects of weak morning light and in the delicious cherry-red and grass-green color notes. But the figure, rather than the swimming atmosphere, is the focal point of the picture. Lautrec was always primarily concerned with human images.

PLATE II

Painted in 1889

THE LAUNDRESS

Collection Dortu, Le Vésinet, France

Oil, 36⅝ x 29½"

There is a precedent for this painting in Degas' *Two Laundresses* of 1884. Degas' interest was mainly in composing an exquisite arrangement of pleasing color notes and ballet-like movements. His realism is relatively mild when set against this stark handling. Lautrec's laundress also bears a striking resemblance to a profiled Renoir figure in *The Bathers* of about 1887. What a difference between the sweatshop pallor here and the healthy flush of Renoir's young animal! This laundress is as degraded by work as figures in later cabaret scenes are brutalized by dissipation.

Plate 12. CIRQUE FERNANDO *(commentary in back of book)*

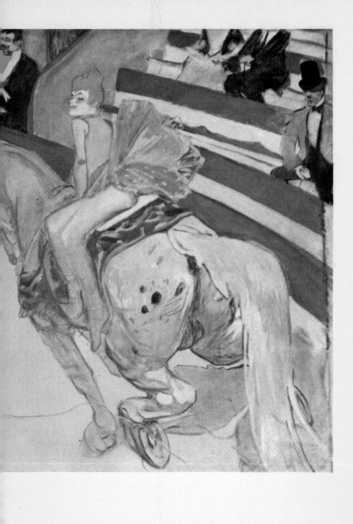

PLATE 13

Painted in 1892

A CORNER IN THE
MOULIN DE LA GALETTE

Collection Chester Dale, New York

Oil, 40 x 39"

This vignette of the sidelines of a music hall is the somber reverse of the coin to the artificial glamor and on-stage atmosphere of large compositions like *At the Moulin Rouge.* The mood is one of unrelieved, funereal disenchantment. The mechanical come-on smile of the rear profile and the business-like authority of the woman in mannish garb who seems about to proposition an apathetic customer represent Lautrec at his least charitable.

PLATE 14

Painted in 1892

LA GOULUE ENTERING
THE MOULIN ROUGE

Collection Dr. and Mrs. David M. Levy, New York

Oil, 31½ x 23"

The well-fleshed La Goulue ("The Glutton," in Montmartre argot) was a celebrated star of the dance hall and the archetype of the Naughty Nineties Beef Trust Girl. With his acute theatrical sense, Lautrec felt related to figures of temperament and loved painting them—whether they happened to be public entertainers, great surgeons in the operating theater, or circus acrobats. He presents La Goulue ironically as a bizarre hussy but gives her a certain insolent grandeur. His more spectacular portraits like this one—all fine nerve and cold fire—have a way of summoning up the portraiture of Goya and El Greco.

PLATE 15

Painted in 1890

AT THE MOULIN DE LA GALETTE

The Art Institute of Chicago

Oil, 35⅜ x 39⅜"

It is impossible not to think of Renoir's ecstatic treat-
ment of this same subject thirteen years earlier. Renoir
sets his figures in the open air, caressing them with a
silky, sun-flecked light. His women are radiant and
his men, ardently attentive. Lautrec's scene is placed
indoors. The bad, shaded illumination is demoraliz-
ing. The onlookers are predatory and wear guarded
expressions. Dancers cavort on the treadmill of pleasure with only an automatic abandon. Although it is true
the clientele of the music hall had changed for the
worse in the intervening years, the shift in interpre-
tation between paintings is symptomatic. A gorgeous
century of progress had begun to break up.

detail of plate 15 (please lift flap)

PLATE 16

Painted in 1892

AT THE MOULIN ROUGE:
THE START OF THE QUADRILLE

National Gallery of Art, Washington
(Chester Dale Collection, Loan)
Oil, 23½ x 21¾"

In one of Montmartre's famous cabarets two non-professional dancers are deftly characterized. One, dim and hesitating, the other at the alert, they face each other across the floor like fencers, awaiting the opening bars of the music. The Moulin Rouge was a scene of popular dancing as well as a showplace for professional song and dance stars like La Goulue, Jane Avril, and Yvette Guilbert whose silhouettes and vital gestures Lautrec memorialized.

PLATE 17

Painted in 1893

M. BOILEAU AT THE CAFE

Cleveland Museum of Art
(Hinman B. Hurlbut Collection)
Oil, 31½ x 25⅝"

Boileau was a yellow journalist of the period. Over-dressed, with the visage of a suckling pig and a manner of self-importance, he has an unwholesome air, reinforced by the lugubrious color scheme. In the glass of absinthe in the foreground Lautrec has hit off a remarkable lyrical contrast; it shines like a pale, sea-green jewel, leavening the impression of human dinginess with a strange, exotic poetry.

Plate 18. A LA MIE (*commentary in back of book*)

PLATE 19

Painted in 1894

LA VISITE: RUE DES MOULINS

Collection Chester Dale, New York

Oil, 31¾ x 21¼"

In alluring veils of color the artist treats the least alluring of themes: two prostitutes lining up for medical inspection. Lautrec's feeling for contrasting human types—and perhaps an unconscious deviltry—made him set off a shopworn prostitute with a fairly jaunty one. He explores the theme of opposition by ingeniously contrasting electric and sedative colors, crisp and nerveless line in the respective coiffures and in the two chemises. Often Lautrec's choicest ironies are reserved for articles of dress.

PLATE 20

Painted in 1892

AT THE MOULIN ROUGE

The Art Institute of Chicago

Oil, 47½ x 55¼"

This is one of Lautrec's assured masterpieces. The illumination is so intense and the color so luxurious that there is a lyrical release into fantasy—into an enchanted aquarium world where figures drift in a dream. A garish music-hall scene becomes legend. Using the bold diagonal of the balustrade to check the arabesque of circulating figures, and the device of picking out incident with a spotlight are Degas stunts. The outlines of the two women in the foreground, however, have an energy that suggests Daumier's generous contours rather than Degas' careful edges. The pair of gentlemen in the left background in derby and top hat are the artist and his cousin, Dr. Gabriel Tapié de Céleyran.

detail of plate 20 (please lift flap)

PLATE 21

Painted in 1894

WOMAN FIXING HER STOCKING

The Museum of Albi, France
Oil and gouache, 23⅝ x 16⅞″

Lautrec periodically went to live and sketch in the brothels and astonished his more solemn social connections and creditors by receiving them there. As an artist inspired in part by the naturalist movement, he was loath to make any class distinctions about his subjects. And he was driven to observe them in their local setting, according to naturalist precepts. He enlivened the stolid descriptions of writers like Zola, however, with personal fantasy, and for their reforming zeal substituted a spirit of comic irony. This sketch is a vital note made on the spot, one of the many out of which later studio paintings were fashioned.

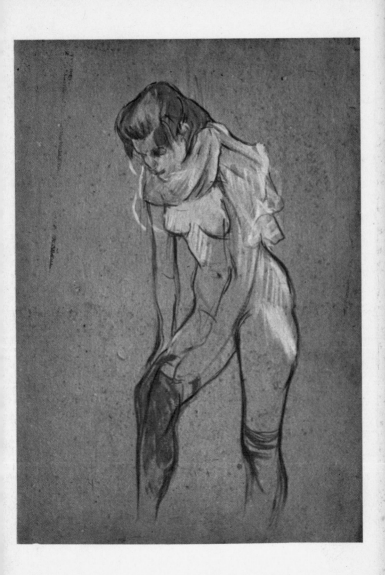

PLATE 22

Painted in 1896

THE TOILETTE

The Louvre, Museum of Impressionism, Paris

Oil, 25⅝ x 20⅞"

Lautrec's mature paintings are of a striking originality. But he borrowed pictorial ideas freely and was saturated in the art of his time. This picture suggests more than one hard look at Degas, the artist he admired most. The ungainly attitude of the nude, dramatized by the tilted floor plane, and the shade of rust in the hair recall that artist's pastel, *The Tub,* executed ten years before. The pellucid blue tonality may have been siphoned off from a Cézanne Provençal landscape. Nevertheless, the picture remains a vital, individual creation.

PLATE 23

Painted in 1897

THE GRAND LOGE

Collection Mettler, St. Gallen, Switzerland

Oil, 21¼ x 18¼"

An inveterate theatergoer, Lautrec divided his artistic interest between the players and the audience. He did many lithographs and this one painting of figures in the stalls. Here he poses a group in attitudes of comic dignity. The rapidly diminishing perspective of the four stalls and the rising curves of the partitions give the occupants an air of being ludicrously suspended in mid-air. The composition is daring but most successful. The figures are concentrated in the left half of the painting, but the red borders and the tilted chair pull them back into equilibrium.

PLATE 24

Painted in 1894

SALON IN THE RUE DES MOULINS

The Museum of Albi, France

Pastel, 51⅛ x 43¼"

In the most important of his brothel scenes Lautrec's waggish humor and bold design play back and forth in many wry contrasts. The figure in the high-necked white dress, possibly the madam, is a picture of official good form, while beside her relaxes a trollop, all but yawning with boredom and fatigue. One of the drollest touches is placing the girls in the background against a dressy, ornate molding, to underline their immodesty. As delicately as a Japanese print, this masterful composition is balanced on the diagonal of the extended leg.

detail of plate 24 (please lift flap)

Painted in 1896

CHILPERIC

Collection Mr. and Mrs. John Hay Whitney, New York

Oil, $57\frac{1}{2}$ x $57\frac{7}{8}$"

Lautrec mixes a sharp appreciation of the human comedy with liberal dashes of fantasy. In this he relates to an honorable French tradition of comic exaggeration. He crosses tracks at some point with the eighteenth-century poet, La Fontaine. La Fontaine's sage verse invests a plausible animal kingdom with mortal flaws and human foibles, and the effect is ludicrous. Lautrec's characterizations are psychologically realistic, in details of gesture and in dress, but his sense of the ridiculous finds excuses for continually adding more fanciful trimmings to the human image until quite another animal emerges. Here he gives to Marcelle Lender, the star of the operetta *Chilperic,* the aspect of a gaudy and predatory jungle bird.

detail of plate 25 (please lift flap)

PLATE 2 6

Painted in 1897

MADAME BERTHE BADY

The Museum of Albi, France

Oil, 27⅛ x 22⅞"

Lautrec sometimes engages our attention by using color as an irritant. Instead of employing local color, he works freely in broad, expressive areas to dramatize mood. In this portrait of an actress he extracts disturbing dissonances from clashing mauves, indigos, and bilious greens. The color is as out of sorts as the sitter seems to be; her wry, nervous pucker is taken up in the clenched hand and re-echoed in the writhing pattern of the white brocade in the dress. The sickish air of the portrait may be a humorous side commentary on Mme. Bady's stage personality. At the time she was starring in a play called *The Leper*.

PLATE 27

Painted in 1899

PRIVATE ROOM AT "LE RAT MORT"

Courtauld Institute of Art, London

Oil, 21¾ x 18⅛"

Painted just after Lautrec's mental collapse, this work is still uncertain in style. The savage handling and violent lighting prophesy modern Expressionism. "Le Rat Mort" was one of the few smart, expensive restaurants in the picturesque "popular" quarter of Montmartre, apparently famous for its private dining rooms.

PLATE 28

Painted in 1900

THE MODISTE

The Museum of Albi, France

Oil, 24 x 19"

After a severe breakdown in 1899 produced by alcoholism and overwork, Lautrec painted few pictures to the time of his death, two years later. In this one his hand has regained its cunning but there is a slackness of style that indicates how badly his powers had deteriorated. The mood of the picture is strangely pacific, and there is even a certain nobility in the head, as if the experience of suffering had softened Lautrec's waspish wit.

Plate 29. AMBASSADEURS: ARISTIDE BRUANT. *1892. Poster*
Museum of Modern Art, New York

Plate 30.   REINE DE JOIE. 1892. Poster
Museum of Modern Art, New York

Plate 31. OSCAR WILDE. *1895. Essence*
Collection Durand-Ruel, Paris

Plate 32. HEAD OF A YOUNG WOMAN. *1898. Sanguine*
The Louvre, Paris

Plate 33. CHOCOLAT DANCING IN ACHILLE'S BAR. *1896. Pencil*
Collection Ludwig Charell, New York

Plate 34. THE ENRAGED COW. *1896. Poster*
Collection Ludwig Charell, New York

Plate 35. WOMAN WASHING (*from* ELLES). *1896. Color lithograph*
Museum of Modern Art, New York

Plate 36. FEMALE CLOWN (*from* ELLES). *1896. Color lithograph*
Collection Ludwig Charell, New York

Plate 37. A RIDE IN THE COUNTRY. *1897. Color lithograph. Collect*

Plate 38. **THE JOCKEY.** *1899. Lithograph*
Collection Ludwig Charell, New York

Plate 39. AT THE CIRCUS. *1899. Colored pencil*
Collection Ludwig Charell, New York

Painted in 1888

CIRQUE FERNANDO

The Art Institute of Chicago
(Gift of Tiffany and Margaret Blake)
Oil, 38¾ x 63½"

A knack for blending psychological and formal incident is one of Lautrec's greatest gifts. Here the ring-
master's cracking whip is like an electrical impulse,
connecting his smart stage direction and the brilliant,
theatrical grimace the bareback rider obliges with. The
whip also figures as a spoke to the hub of the ring-
master's tense silhouette, driving the circular composition in a slow, controlled arc. The decorative shapes
and expressive outlines probably derive from Japanese prints; the influence of Degas—and of photog-
raphy—is clear in the stress on "the moment" of action.

Painted in 1891

A LA MIE

Museum of Fine Arts, Boston

Oil, 19¾ x 27½"

This vision of dissoluteness is so extreme that it becomes pure burlesque. Actually it was painted from a
posed photograph of a pleasant-looking couple who
were friends of the artist. How different is the relative
refinement and cool classical reserve of Degas'
Absinthe, which probably inspired the composition.
Lautrec delineates his most debased and dispiriting
types with a riot of gaudy color. His colors have a freedom and expressiveness apart from representational
aims that anticipate modern abstract art.

BIOGRAPHICAL NOTES

1864   Henri de Toulouse-Lautrec *(to-LOOSE lo-TREK)* born November 24 at Albi in southern France. Father, Count Alphonse de Toulouse-Lautrec, was head of one of France's oldest noble families; mother, Countess Adele, was the Count's first cousin.

1878–79   Two accidents to his legs, which remain stunted.

1881–84   Studies art in Paris under Princeteau, a deaf-mute painter of animal subjects; later enters studios of the academicians Bonnat and Cormon; meets Degas, Van Gogh.

1885   Moves into studio in rue Tourlaque; remains there for thirteen years painting and drawing the cabarets, circuses, bistros, and brothels of Montmartre.

1889–92   Contributes to Salon des Indépendents; first posters, which place him squarely in the public eye, and first color prints.

1893–97   First exhibitions of his work in Paris; visits Brussels, London (where he meets Wilde and Beardsley), Holland, Spain, and Portugal.

1899   Failing health; is confined in a sanatorium near Paris as consequence of severe alcoholism.

1901   Final breakdown; stays with his mother at Malrômé where he dies of a stroke, September 9.

SOME OTHER BOOKS
ABOUT TOULOUSE-LAUTREC

Douglas Cooper. *Toulouse-Lautrec* (Portfolio Editions of The Library of Great Painters). New York, Harry N. Abrams, 1952

Loys Delteil. *Le Peintre-graveur Illustré* (Volumes X and XI). Paris, Delteil, 1920
(Complete catalogue of Lautrec's graphic work)

Theodore Duret. *Lautrec*. Paris, Bernheim-Jeune, 1920
(Lautrec's art and life interpreted by the art critic who was an intimate of his circle)

Maurice Joyant. *Henri de Toulouse-Lautrec, Peintre.* Paris, Floury, 1926
(The standard biography by the painter's closest friend and dealer)

Gerstle Mack. *Toulouse-Lautrec*. New York, Alfred A. Knopf, 1938
(The popular English biography, with a full account of the Montmartre music-hall life Lautrec drew on)

SOME OPINIONS
IN NEWSPAPERS OF THE TIME

La Vie Artistique, Paris, 1891: "M. de Toulouse-Lautrec presents scenes in equivocal surroundings with a mocking wilfulness, in dirty colors, from which emerge horrible creatures, the larvae of vice and poverty."

Gustave Geoffroy, *La Justice,* Paris, 1893: "The degradation and horror are undeniable . . . Yet he remains a sincere artist, his pitiless observation is aware of the beauty of life, and the philosophy of vice which he sometimes proclaims with irritating ostentation nevertheless acquires, by the power of his drawing and the depth of his probing, the value, for purposes of demonstration, of a lesson in moral surgery."

La Vie Artistique, Paris, 1896: "There is in Lautrec an innate sense of caricature which it would be a great pity to repress, because it is rich in its exposure of social pretensions and moral blemishes."

The Art Journal, London, 1898: ". . . one of the most extreme followers of Degas. His subjects are unlikely to commend themselves to old ladies, but their execution is undeniably clever."

The Daily Chronicle, London, 1898: "M. de Toulouse-Lautrec typifies the most genuine phase of modern French art—the cult of vulgarity and ugliness . . . Technically, at times, he is magnificent."